# *A*
# *Writer's*
# *Wisdom*

Jan Marquart

Jan Marquart CEO and Founder of
About the Author Network
www.AboutTheAuthorNetwork.com
jan_marquart@yahoo.com
www.JanMarquart.com

# Other Books by the Author

*Write to Heal*

*The Mindful Writer, Still the Mind, Free the Pen*

*The Basket Weaver, a Novel*

*Kate's Way, a Novel*

*Echoes from the Womb, a Book for Daughters*

*Voices from the Land*

*The Breath of Dawn, a Journey of Everyday Blessings*

*How to Write From Your Heart (booklet)*

*How to Write Your Own Memoir (booklet)*

*A Manual on How to Deal With a Bully in the Workplace*

*Cracked Open, a Book of Poems*

*Writing, when all is said and done, is an attempt to understand one's own circumstances and to clarify the confusion of existence, including insecurities that do not torment normal people, only chronic nonconformists, many of whom end up as writers having failed in other undertakings.*

Isabel Allenda

# Dedication

This book is dedicated to writers who have persisted at all costs, dreamers who envision taking up the pen, and faithful followers who stand on the sidelines cheering them on.

*We carry with us every story we have ever heard, and every story we have ever lived.*

Rachel Naomi Remen

# Acknowledgment

I acknowledge the writers quoted in this book for his/her brilliant account of a writer's wisdom and what it means to write about one's life with boldness.

*To me a book is a message from the gods to*
*mankind; or, if not, should never be published at all.*
Aleister Crowley

# WELCOME!

*Did you know that close to 240 million Americans, (81%), believe a book lives within them?*

*Roughly 48 million people, (20%), ever hope to actually get started on their ideas.*

*Fewer than 2% of those who start a book ever finish it.*

Which part of these statistics are you? What are the obstacles keeping you from writing? Write about them and bring them to the surface so you can better understand what is holding you back. Obstacles can be anything from fear, self-doubt, people who might be hurt, to procrastination.

Realize that you have the power to tear up your written work, burn it, bury it, or publish it. First write and then decide.

We can answer the call of the wild within or run like hell - but the worse thing we can do is not respond at all. I encourage you to write even if you think someone *might* not like it or might be hurt by it.

I understand the intention not to want to hurt anyone but that still doesn't mean you should not write. It doesn't make you a mean or terrible person if you write and someone is upset by it. People like to hide from the truth, theirs and others. And that is exactly why writers are different. We are iconoclastic thinkers. We like to take a path different from what others choose. We want to think about something from another angle, explore the other side of an idea, and find a way to make life meaningful. We want to speak the unmentionable and do the unthinkable. We want to clean the closets of secrets and get the cobwebs out of our minds.

The fabulous quotes in this book are selected specifically to inspire, embolden, and guide you to stay on the writer's well-trod road.

Like most travels, the writing journey comes with beautiful vistas, deep valleys, rainy days, thunder, lightning, blazing suns, seasons, and flashbacks. The writing life is quite simply put, another aspect of life. We start out eager, we get lost, we find our way, we find something we like, we find things we don't like, we get lost again, we begin again, we constantly learn about who we are until eventually we find our way to the destination.

Writers want to fill lives with romance, suspense, thrills, help, and salvation and they know that no matter what comes out on the page it will heal, transform, teach, entertain, and offer ways to improve humanity one life at a time.

I have organized the following author quotes into categories that answer some of the ten fundamental questions I have been asked over the years. I hope they help you keep your pen moving.

Jan, CEO and Founder of About the Author Network

Note: Most of the quotes below were pulled from books I've read, some were extracted from online sites.

*If you wish to be a writer, write.*
Epictetus

# Table of Contents

# Question 1

**What if I have no stories to write?**

Really? Is that absolutely true?

It is true that you have stories. Your entire life is made up of stories. That's how we live. Each day is something new. Perhaps you went somewhere you've never been before, had an enlightened moment, or met an interesting person.

You will never write if you believe you have no stories. So, here is how you get over this: write *anyway.* Write about what you had for breakfast. How did it taste? Did you yearn for something else to eat?

Even if it were true that you have nothing that seems worthy of being written by anyone else's standards, if you want to write, you have to write, *anyway*.

The false belief that you have no stories to write steals the truth of your life.

*The scariest moment is always just before you start.*
Stephen King

You make it to the chair, now what? You have a knot in your stomach and your mind is frozen like a Popsicle. But what exactly has you frozen? Ask yourself, what else in life has this effect over you? What else makes you freeze up when you think of doing it? Fear? Humiliation? Shame? This is the perfect place to begin to write.

The mind knows how to trick you to believe there is danger when there isn't. Write down all your thoughts and see what comes out.

Do not give in to the misdiagnosis w*riter's block* because it is a man-made label. By itself, there is no such thing. It is just the mind telling you it has stopped to get your attention – so – pay attention. Telling the truth can be frightening. Is that what you are about to do?

Remember, you are in charge. Lasso the truth, and hang on for dear life. Fear or no fear.

Then go have a bowl of your favorite ice cream. Writing celebrations are important.

Celebrate each page!

*The first draft of anything is shit.*

Ernest Hemingway

Don't let this scare you. Just because you finally got the story on the page doesn't mean it is worthy of an award nor does it mean the show mustn't go on. It does, however, mean that you have written something to work with. So, get to work!

Writers often think that just because their stories have lived in their minds for a long time that they should be born into perfectly written masterpieces. This is delusional. Once the story gets onto the page it is seen for what it is. And it is undoubtedly quite unfinished.

Every author will attest to throwing away beginning chapters, first drafts, or even the second. It is okay. When it is time to let go of something that doesn't work, let go. Writers cannot afford the luxury of fighting this. Amy Tan threw out the first 122 pages of The Joy Luck Club.

Writers can certainly hoard their unwanted paragraphs and pages and tuck them into another story later down the line. So hoard if you want; just don't put them where they don't belong simply because you have become sentimental about them.

Go to writer's conferences or follow blogs and newsletters to understand the writing process. Write – let go – write – let go – eventually something will come out that you can keep and hold onto.

Just get your stories on the page.

*Being a writer is a very peculiar sort of a job: it's always you versus a blank sheet of paper (or a blank screen) and quite often the blank piece of paper wins.*

Neil Gaiman

Anyone who writes knows this is true. Stories have a way of taking you in new directions. It is not the same as other jobs where we get an assignment and stay true to the project. Stories can shift in mid-stream, re-direct our messages, and give characters new idiosyncrasies. Like the Velveteen Rabbit, our stories are like toys that become real.

Find other writers with whom to discuss this scary and wonderful phenomenon. Stay connected to those who know the process.

Laugh, cry, eat, and plant flowers.

*Tomorrow may be hell, but today was a good writing day,*
*and on the good writing days nothing else matters.*
Neil Gaiman

The authentic voice of the muse can feel like a first love. Savor those moments for those are the moments that will keep you writing through cold winters. You could find yourself throwing out tomorrow what you have written today, but for today, they are precious because they took you another step deeper into your story. The more truthful you write from the voice of your inner being, the more love you will develop for the voice that comes through your pen.

The more love you develop the more fun you will have and the more fun you have the more resilient you become to tough times. The more resilient you become the more persistent you become to finishing your writing project. See where is this going?

Voila – your stories are published!

*If you want to really hurt your parents, and you don't have the nerve to be gay, the least you can do is go into the arts. I'm not kidding. The arts are not a way to make a living. They are a very human way of making life more bearable.*
Kurt Vonnegut

Creativity is our greatest healer. Who says we can't use our pens to re-create a healed and happy life? Who says we can't write our stories to meet our imagination? Who says our stories have to please everyone?

Learn ways to manage those who give you a difficult time. Make the villains in your life characters in your novels. Even terrible people can make wonderful stories.

Stay connected to writers to learn some of these amazing methods.

*So what? All writers are lunatics!*
                    Cornelia Funke

Of course writers are lunatics, who else would go deep into the darkness of existence just to come up with one sentence of truth and then, of all things, spend a month editing it? Writers live on the edge. Where else can they find the revelations of life -- certainly not where life is comfortable! Whether the story is one of self-help or nightmarish horror go deep into the darkness because that is where the flicker of light lives. There you will find your best stories.

Create a circle of people who understand the need to live on the edge and make them your safe place. There are more of them around than you might think.

*Perhaps I write for no one. Perhaps for the same person children are writing for when they scrawl their names in the snow.*

Margaret Atwood

Be that child who writes on the white page like making an angel in deep snow. Who are you making a snow angel for? Well, I'm here to tell you, it doesn't matter.

If you write for golfers then maybe golfers will read it. Or just perhaps a football player will read it and become a golfer. Other than trying to make a good match for publishing, all I can say is, don't worry about your audience. Just write. Tell your story and deal with where to send it later. The *Writer's Market* is replete with resources. Get a copy of it. They come out each year.

As far as who wants to read your stories, people are not that predictable. It is impossible to know who will want to read what you wrote and where they will be when they read it. Write from the truth that lives in your experience of being human and the rest will fall into place. What other point of view could you have?

Writers make up enough excuses on their own. Don't let some imaginary group of people dictate that you have to write for a particular group.

You never know who will pick up your book in an airport or train station. I got a call from a woman one morning who wanted to tell me that she loved my memoir and she found it in a Laundromat. Books seem to have their own destinies; they land in the laps of those who need them.

*Why did I write? Because I found life unsatisfactory.*
Tennessee Williams


Take an event that happened to you, one that you didn't like and write about it – give it a higher purpose, a better history, a desired value. Write a beautiful future for your painful experience. Pain can lead us to revelations and enlightenments. View the painful experience from a place of distance and wisdom. Who says writing about pain only creates more pain?

Years ago I watched an interview with a famous female novelist. She wrote her next protagonist as the man she always wanted instead of the one she had. Soon after she completed her manuscript she divorced her husband then found the man she wrote about and married him.

Like getting dressed in your comfy clothes, let your pen make you feel better.

*Writing is the only thing that when I do it, I don't feel I
should be doing something else.*
                                    Gloria Steinem

When we write from a sense of sacred creativity how can
we not feel that writing is the most essential thing we can
do?

Write authentically. Know what life is giving you. Know
that you can write about your life in a way that brings you
a feeling of satisfaction. Writing is an intimate way to
express yourself.

Know that you can learn from your pen because it is eager
to teach you what lies underneath your experiences.
Writing glues fragmented experiences together. It
transforms us into a sense of wholeness.

This is the moment when dancing is a natural physical
follow-up – well – dancing and eating cheesecake.

*Writing is a way of talking without being interrupted.*
Jules Renard

Most of us can say that there have been times when we replayed arguments in our heads trying to defend ourselves in order to create a wanted outcome. When our minds fight for us we give them our full attention.

Why not do the same when you write? Put a note on your door: WRITING - DO NOT DISTURB. Let yourself have an uninterrupted conversation with your private inner story.

Be careful, though, the critical antagonist of your life will want to sit on your shoulder and tell you what not to write and make you scared to have your own company as a fabulous companion.

Don't listen to it. Write a dialogue with it and make sure you win the argument. Then get busy writing your desired story.

*A poem is a contribution to reality. The world is never the same once a good poem has been added to it.*

Dylan Thomas

That's the part of writing that makes writers love the pen, *i.e.*, the part that draws a difference between the world we live in and the world we imagine.

Each word is powerful. Think about it. If I wrote, *this is a sour orange*, would it feel the same as, *this is a sweet orange*? Sentences laced with the senses and emotions are powerful. This poem by Jimmy Santiago Baca speaks to an experience that shifts perspectives.

*Where the tree had stood*
*a silver waterfall of sky now poured down.*
*Still air. Red dusk. I felt I had just killed*
*an old man.*

published in *Breaking Bread With the Darkness*, Book 1, *The Esai Poems* p. 10

Jimmy Santiago Baca is a powerful memoirist. This poem changed how I think about  felled trees.

When our emotional visions are put into words they magnify the aspects of life that sit underneath the surface. Be willing to go there.

*Find out the reason that commands you to write; see whether it has spread its roots into the very depth of your heart; confess to yourself you would have to die if you were forbidden to write.*

Rainer Maria Rilke

When Tolstoy got too sick to write he dictated his ideas to his daughter so she could write them for him. That is a true writer. For anyone of such desire, writing is like breathing – the call dies only when the writer takes its last breath. The stories, however, live on forever. That's what a true writer hopes for.

To write is to honor, make sacred, give value, spread a message, enjoy, love, and share.

Spread your stories, even if the people around you aren't interested in them. There are six billion other people in the world that might be.

*But my life is, I believe, excellent fodder for fiction.*
Amy Tan

## Question 2

**What do I do if people get angry at me for writing my stories?**

People? What people? Whoever they are, do you really want to give them power over your creative voice?

If you examine your life up to this point, I'm sure you can come up with names of people who threatened to be upset with you no matter what you did. Did you always let them bully you into avoiding things you wanted to do just to please them? Do you want to live your life that way? There are too many bullies who don't want people to tell the truth. Bullies are insecure, jealous, mean-spirited, small minded, and usually mediocre. That's their problem. Don't make it yours too.

Sometimes it seems everyone is looking for someone to vent their anger on and writers who want to speak up are great targets. I'm not sure exactly why that is, but these are the people who are toxic, not only to your writing life, but to you as a spiritually growing human being as well.

What if people become angry with you after you write your story? Then what? I know that seems like an unfair question because having someone angry at you is usually an unwanted experience. However, if someone threatens that they will become angry at you for writing, then I promise you they are already angry about something and are simply looking for a place to put it.

Watch your mind here. What is it thinking and believing? What emotions are being created over something that is essentially in your power to control? My suggestion is to write anyway. Start small – perhaps a few sentences then stop and examine how you feel. Write another sentence. Examine your reaction. Understand your mind and how it works, how it holds you back, how your fear and shame take over. Examine the vulnerability that emerges. Now write about that. By knowing the workings of your mind, your world, and your part in it, you change.

Sometimes we outgrow the people in our lives.

Good!

We are not human to stand still.

*Be yourself; everyone else is already taken.*
Oscar Wilde

Don't try to emulate any writer, not even your favorite. Sit quietly, listen, then listen again, then listen some more, and write out everything your voice says, the way it says it, without censoring. You know when you have written from your own voice because no matter how it sounds you will feel as if you have just met God.

Writing is not for sissies.

Then call a friend and laugh.

*In three words I can sum up everything I've learned about life: it goes on.*

Robert Frost

Let's speak about those feared rejection letters for a minute. Too many writers think rejections are the end of their writing career. Writers need to be more like the country western song – *when you're going through hell keep on going- don't look back - if you're scared don't show it.*

Some writers cover their entire offices with rejection letters, some nurse them like war wounds, others throw them in the recycling bin and wait for better results.

My suggestion: find another agent and write a more powerful query letter or book proposal. I bet JK Rowling is glad she didn't give up after the twelfth rejection. The thirteenth was her lucky charm. *If You Meet the Buddha on the Road Kill Him* received 122 rejections in the late 70's. Good thing the authors did not give up. It is still a bestseller. *Chicken Soup for the Soul* received 144 rejections.

Just keep writing, learn all you can about your story and how best to craft it, then put it back out in the world. Refuse to accept anger, judgment, and abandonment.

Other writers can help with the normalcy of this phenomenon– stay connected to the writing community. And remember Robert Frost's words: *life goes on.*

*Better to write for yourself and have no public, than to write for the public and have no self.*
                                    Cyril Connolly

The pen doesn't care who its audience is. All it knows is the feeling of being on stage. And it knows the feeling of having someone else steal its lines because the writer has betrayed it. Always be authentic when you write or you will break your own heart. If you can't write your story according to how the self knows it, there is no point.

Each writer must write according to its own experience. That is the only way readers see the authentic voice.

You can't please everyone.

*If you expect to succeed as a writer, rudeness should be the second-to-least of your concerns. The least of all should be polite society and what it expects. If you intend to write as truthfully as you can, your days as a member of polite society are numbered, anyway.*

Stephen King

Maybe it's unfortunate or maybe it's just necessary, but when you write your personal stories you must not stress about whose toes you are stepping on. I don't mean that you should set out to be vindictive, slanderous, or unkind. I do mean that you must set your intention to be boldly honest and write nothing less.

No one likes to be socially outcast, but writers have no choice. A lack of honesty is never politically correct. The minute a writer tries to co-dependently make the reader happy, she gets depressed, just like in real life.

I wish I could spare you writer's pain because life can be painful enough. I'm so sorry. I've lost friends over pieces I've written, not because I had cast them in an awful light, but because they wanted me to applaud them more than I did. Even with the best of intentions, they got upset.

It hurt me. There is no way around it. But writing is just like life. You can't make everyone happy all the time.

*There are only two mistakes one can make along the road to truth; not going all the way, and not starting.*
Buddha

If you do nothing else but write three words a day – by the time the year is out you will have written 1,095 words. One tiny step is all it takes to start the journey. Continuing with each step will finally get you to the finished result.

Years ago I lived with a man who watched me each morning write in my journal. He usually commented that he wished he could write every day too. Even after I bought him a journal to kick start the process, I never saw him write.

One morning he remarked that even if he wrote the worse junk, he'd still feel good because he had written. But as I drank tea and wrote, he drank coffee and wished. There was no way he was going to allow himself to write junk, he was too much of a perfectionist. His mind was always tormenting him.

Often he'd sit for hours trying to decide what to write on a friend's birthday card. He'd write what he wanted to say on scratch paper first, then edit it, edit it, and edit it. He was so particular that if he didn't have a blue flair pen to write with, he wouldn't even write a check in the grocery line. Instead he'd race to the stationery aisle to buy a blue flair pen. But perfectionism is just another form of self-abuse. How can anyone write anything with that mindset?

How is your mind interrupting your writing process? Is your mind angry that you are not perfect?

# Question 3

**What if I'm not creative enough to write?**

Who says you have to be creative and who says you aren't? Everyone writes differently. Creativity comes in all fashions like shoes. Read the many genres in the bookstore and you will see what I mean. Is a writer more creative if she has written a novel versus a business man who has come up with a great idea to make money?

Do you have a fantasy about how you *should* write that is getting in your way? Write that conflict out. Expose it to the light so you can examine whether it is truthful.

If a burning desire to write still haunts you, join a writing group and talk to the people in the group about what you are going through. Ask if they ever felt the same way. My guess is that they did - somewhere along the line.

Being *enough* as a creative person or *enough* as a writer is no different. There is never enough to enough. Writers are always trying to grow their creativity level.

Just start. You won't know how creative you are until you start. Stephen King spends months working on a first sentence or paragraph. Does that mean he is not creative?

*"Perfectionism is a refusal to let yourself move ahead."*
Julia Cameron

Perfectionism is another form of self-abuse. Academic insults and personal criticisms can be so imbedded in our minds that soon we can't even hear our own voices. We believe that we must be perfect in order for our critical and judgmental voices to leave us alone. The truth is that they need to leave us alone, anyway.

Once I watched an interview on TV with Maya Angelou. She was examining her old original manuscripts that lay open in a glass case. The interviewer complimented her books when suddenly she gasped and pointed. She found an error and wanted to edit the book which had been published decades ago.

Sometimes it is just time to hit the print button.

Then go buy yourself something nice and celebrate.

*Writing is perhaps the greatest of human inventions, binding together people, citizens of distant epochs, who never knew one another. Books break the shackles of time — proof that humans can work magic.*

Carl Sagan

The blank page is nothing until a writer marks it up with words to greet the edge of her mind and create like God.

There is nothing more to say about that. Describe a monarch butterfly lifting off a leaf and you can feel what the white page allows you to do.

In the 70's in Santa Cruz, California there was a young man named Bert Glick. He was so determined to be a poet that he copied his poems at Kinkos and stapled them into small chapbooks, then stood on the corner selling them for $2. I bought every one. That was way before self-published authors had options for professional publishing.

If he could stand on the corner to sell his books, you can too.

*A writer is a person who cares what words mean, what they say, how they say it. Writers know words are their way towards truth and freedom, and so they use them with care, with thought, with fear, with delight. By using words well they strengthen their souls.*

Ursula K. Le Guin

Each of us is a seeker of something. Books are one of the greatest resources for wisdom. Words for the writer are as important as colors to the interior designer. They should never be taken for granted. A contractor would not use a one inch nail to hammer a two by four in the wall of a kitchen. Nor should a writer use a word without making sure its meaning is correctly used. A cook would not use an egg where basil is needed. A seamstress would not try to sew with a knitting needle. The words writers use are important for the meaning of their stories.

Go to a bookstore and read first sentences to learn the most powerful way to begin. Notice those books that you surrender back to the shelf and those that make you want to read further.

**Rainbow the Editor**

I had a cat
who sat on my lap
as I read manuscripts
aloud.

Quietly she'd rest
her paw on my palm
and listen.

No one believed me
when I said
she'd lift her head
with a screechy meow

when my story
missed a beat.

Friends laughed.
Authors doubted.
Children wanted to know - *was it true?*

Could it be
that Rainbow the cat
was my editor?

Yes, I'd say -- it's true.

Jan Marquart
(published in *Cracked Open, A Book of Poems*, 2013)

*For it would seem - her case proved it - that we write, not with the fingers, but with the whole person.*
Virginia Woolf

When a writer writes from the connection of its inner essence nothing else matters in that moment. The power comes from the confidence in saying what needs to be said from the depths of authenticity and no one lives there but you.

The energy in a written piece is what connects writers with readers. I've often edited manuscripts in which writers want to describe a powerful experience but fall short of the goal. When I mentioned it to them they got frustrated. They hoped their readers would miraculously get the message. But this process doesn't just happen. It must be designed carefully with words and emotional inner corrections.

Sometimes experiences are painful or take too much energy to be written from a deep place. Just the same, the writer *must* go down deep or the message will be as shallow as the writer's effort.

Have some friends over and read your work to them. They will let you know where you fall short. Go to a writing group. Talk about the place you have trouble entering and get some help.

*Let the world burn through you. Throw the prism light,*
*white hot, on paper.*
                                    Ray Bradbury


New writers think they should be able to write everything
neat, organized and well written. Not so. At the initial
writing it is important to forget all the rules and just get
the words onto the paper. The birth of new stories on the
page will often come out like a tornado swirling memories,
emotions, and the human condition all over the place.

Writers have no storm cellar. Just the urge to keep editing
until every word is in its place and the feeling of the piece
sits *just right.*

*It's not: I jumped in, and it was cold. No. It was cold, and I jumped in. Always arrange a sentence so you appear to be fearless, when in fact you are far less than fearless—you are clueless.*

Jarod Kintz

Readers look to writers to take them where they cannot go alone. They want writers to be brave, courageous, and tireless in finding solutions to problems. They want writers to venture into the truth, to rid the world of demons, to tackle the difficult questions, because the reader wants the writer to show them the way.

A writer cannot afford to disappoint its readers. Readers expect the life raft, the rock to hold onto, the pocket of hope to breathe safely in.

Creativity is a means of problem solving.

*This most of all: ask yourself in the most silent hour of your night: must I write? Dig into yourself for a deep answer. And if this answer rings out in assent, if you meet this solemn question with a strong, simple "I must," then build your life in accordance with this necessity; your whole life, even into its humblest and most indifferent hour, must become a sign and witness to this impulse.*

Rainer Maria Rilke

What else is there to say? The process is personal, it is mandatory, it gets you by the jugular until you answer the call, and that call is universal. What if you don't answer the call? Will you be bothered by that inner voice until you act? *Of course!*

The writer has a great burden. He carries the weight of the world on every word. Readers demand it, they unknowingly depend on the writer to tell stories about life, how to get out of problems, how to find true love, how to build a successful life, and so much more.

Answer the call or be haunted.

*Tears are words that need to be written.*
                              Paulo Coelho


Each tear holds its own human story. Some of their stories
speak to sadness or grief. Others speak to joy and
celebration.

Whatever tears say to you, write their meanings and
purpose. Real life is quite creative on its own.

Join a writing group and read all you can. The inner voice
has an important reason to exist.

*If my doctor told me I had only six minutes to live, I wouldn't brood. I'd type a little faster.*

Isaac Asimov

So many books in a writer's head – so little time. Writers do not have time for excuses or to give up their pens.

There are millions of people who like quashing the dreams of others. Why give dream murderers all the power?

Go off into a corner, if you must, and write.

*Fantasy is hardly an escape from reality. It's a way of understanding it.*

Lloyd Alexander

Try as you might there is no way around it – if you write you will become philosophic. You will find your muse. You will hear that annoying inner voice whisper and it will lead you through life wiser but only if you acknowledge it.

Try as you might to take one step out of the real and you will find yourself entering chaos. Go back, listen again, watch the inner movie, then search for the word with the matching energetic vibration.

Witness the trip and keep the pen moving.

## Writer's Life

A writer's life looks
insane to those who
play by the rules

bumping the edge where
normal people won't dare go

flying into storms
without protection, only
words for umbrellas
while the sane prepare with planks and nails

and seeks the pen with burning eyes
when others close theirs
then leaps and flies as
others nestle under
covers to be
safe and warm.

Jan Marquart
(published in *Cracked Open, A Book of Poems*, 2013)

*Write your desires.*

Habakkuk 2:2

# Question 4

**Why can't I write?**

Did you go to school? Do you keep grocery lists? Do you write lists for activities such as birthday parties, weddings, Christmas presents, and more? Then put on your list of things to do: *write.*

Often when people announce that they cannot write they are basically referring to someone else's negative comments. We are impressionable when it comes to our creativity. We take in everything people say and worse, even believe them. I'm here to tell you that you can write.

Make a list of every birthday present you got last year. Now put each present into a sentence. Now make it a paragraph. Keep going – who was there, what were they wearing, did they dance? Grammar is only a concern if you want to publish. Then you can hire an editor or take a class in grammatical correctness. Many of the books written in the 70's were stream of consciousness in which sentences were barely constructed the academic way. If you have something to write, and I know you do, write it. No excuses.

*Can't* is the perfect word to make you *not* do something. Is that how you want to think about your capabilities?

*The only way you can write the truth is to assume that what you set down will never be read. Not by any other person, and not even by yourself at some later date. Otherwise you begin excusing yourself.*

Margaret Atwood

Okay, you have found your desk chair. In front of you is a blank screen and your fingers are correctly leaning against the keys. Now what? Suddenly you feel a knot in your stomach and your head hurts. Fear swells from deep within. Your brain cells beat against your head. You imagine everyone you know throwing your stories into raging fires.

Now imagine that you are sitting on a peaceful island with a large palm tree against your back. You look to the shore and you see hands waving and hear shouts of joy because you have decided to write your stories.

Pick one of the stories in your head. Take a deep breath. You are allowed to feel weak and insecure. All that matters is that the stories burning inside you find the page. And you can write them!

Here is how slow you can take this: you only have to write your stories *one* word at a time - just *one* word.

Drop the mind chatter about the world accepting or rejecting. The computer makes editing easy. There are many people in the world who want to help you with your stories.

Go to: www.AboutTheAuthorNetwork.com and contact an author or two on the site. Contact me as the CEO and Founder. This site is about supporting, networking, completing manuscripts and publishing and to let you know that you are not alone.

*Your intuition knows what to write, so get out of the way.*
Ray Bradbury


Writers often try to talk themselves into organizing what they need to write before anything even gets on paper. They want to make sure nothing spills out of them that isn't perfect.

Vulnerability and shame are a writer's personal nightmares. Step out of the personal fears and just tell it as you want to tell it.

Rely on that deep sense of inner knowing. That is the place where authenticity lives. Learn to surrender to it. There is no point stressing out. Your mind is not the author. Your inner sense is.

After your story is on paper, outline what you have. You will see once you start organizing your story into a structure if something is missing or you have too many pieces.

*Amateurs sit and wait for inspiration, the rest of us just get up and go to work.*

Stephen King

It is foolish to think writing projects will get completed through inspiration alone. No one argues that inspiration is a wonderful and motivational experience, but no author has written solely on inspiration.

Do you wait for inspiration before you go to the office to finish a project? Of course not, if you did you would most likely be fired. So why expect that you will have inspiration each time you write? It doesn't make sense. The writing process is not any different than what we do in the rest of our lives. We just like to think so, for some strange reason. And let this be known: all artists must work hard in order to create.

Like life, there are parts of writing we like and parts we don't, parts we need to learn, and parts that come naturally.

Waiting for anything to happen is a waste of time. Join other writers and get support to keep the pen moving.

*The pages are still blank, but there is a miraculous feeling of the words being there, written in invisible ink and clamoring to become visible.*

Vladimir Nabokov

Writers write in their heads before the words meet the page. They see words forming paragraphs and characters come alive as they mentally create their stories. They conjure characters while cooking dinner, organize dialogue while folding laundry, and prepare plots while cleaning out a closet. Then suddenly when the story becomes so full of life that the writer cannot stand it anymore, it is time to reach for the pen.

Every book comes from imagination. Know when it is time to write, and then write.

Buy a pen of your favorite color.  Make an intimate connection to the tools you need. Make it personal.

Just do it! The readers are waiting for your stories.

*I write entirely to find out what I'm thinking, what I'm looking at, what I see and what it means. What I want and what I fear.*

Joan Didion

Stream of consciousness writing is perfect for witnessing the mind. Write what you know. Write what you don't know. Write about apples and ripe peaches. Write about what you think of your neighbor, God, and the grocery store. See, stories are already inside you.

Get a kaleidoscope and play with perspectives. It just might get you wondering what it would be like to make words out of pictures and words out of the pictures inside you.

All life is plot and character development. You are living what you want to write. Study the details of the writing craft but what it all boils down to is getting words on paper. Everything follows that first step.

This is where the writer meets herself then turns around and introduces herself to readers so they can meet themselves as well.

*All the ideas in the universe can be described by words. Therefore, if you simply take all the words and rearrange them randomly enough times, you're bound to hit upon at least a few great ideas eventually. Sausage donkey swallows flying guillotine, my love assembly line.*

Jarod Kintz

Emotionally, this is a great way to start out. It takes the sting out of having to find the right words before you even begin.

Take your grocery list and make a story out of the items on it. What do those items say about your thinking? What do they say about your lifestyle? We are built for story and story. Every micro-moment of life is a story.

Remember, these are the moments fudge and ice cream were made for. Stress and celebration desire treats.

*The role of a writer is not to say what we can all say, but what we are unable to say.*

Anais Nin


Here is the agony of most writers. To write what we cannot say means there is only one place from which to truly write –the place that holds the word-less essence of our knowledge because it lives in impressions inside experiences.

Take a long walk and get your body moving to shake out the cobwebs then get writing.

*All you have to do is write one true sentence. Write the truest sentence that you know.*

Ernest Hemingway

This sounds easy, doesn't it? After all we know the truth don't we?

I once thought that all strawberries were red until I met someone who showed me a white strawberry. But if I were to ask you what is true for you and only you, would you be able to come up with something?

This is a good exercise to get the writing process flowing and your mind active with rich ideas.

If nothing comes to mind, then write what *isn't* true for you. That might be easier to write because conflict always gets us stirred up.

*There is no greater agony than bearing an untold story inside you.*

Maya Angelou

This statement by Maya Angelou is the best explanation for why writers write than any explanation I've ever heard. After all, it is our stories that unite us with all of humanity and if we don't share them we can feel disconnected.

What drives a person to write his stories?

What is your untold story?

*There is nothing to writing. All you do is sit down at a typewriter and bleed.*

                              Ernest Hemingway

What brings you to your knees? You must go there. Ego and the pen are enemies.

That's why Kleenex and M&M's are so popular. Buy some.

Then let yourself bleed your stories onto the page.

*It is not what you have but what you have lost that links the reader and the writer. The longing to repair loss is in the rhythm and tone of the written piece, not in its words.*

Nuala O'Faolain


It is the experience of being alive that connects people around the world. Our humanity is filled with emotions, teachings, experiences that weave us into one tapestry.

A great many books speak to grief, dying, hardship, and suffering and have become best sellers. It is no surprise.

That's where our lives hold their meanings. Those dark places take us to the light so we can appreciate the value of celebrating.

Share your stories and connect to people.

*I write my thinking. I think by writing. I persist in the belief that I can articulate whatever I think about. Because I persist, I can. Because I know how, I can. By the words I choose, by their sound and sequence and significance, I shape for you new eyes, new ears, a new mind, so that you, reading, listening, say, "Yes, that's what I mean (or see, or think, or hear.)" I write what I mean, what I understand, what I know. This is my work.*

Alice Koller

Watch the flowers, stars, ocean waves, leaves falling from trees – think about their rhythm, how do all these aspects of nature relate to one another? How is nature connected to us?

Write about what a flower looks like, how it smells, how the water ripples, how an old man smiles. Write about the essence of nature in your life, your emotions, your beliefs, and your relationships.

Nature is full of writing opportunities.

*If you can tell stories, create characters, devise incidents, and have sincerity and passion, it doesn't matter a damn how you write.*

Somerset Maugham

# Question 5

**Do you think I can write a book?**

Go into any bookstore. Look at the thousands of books on the shelves. Some of those authors didn't think they could write a book either. When you were two you couldn't dress yourself but by the time you were five you could tie your shoes, pick out your socks, put on your sun bonnet, zipper your sweater, and pull up your pants.

When you were in the first grade you might not have been able to do subtraction but by the fourth grade you could. In grammar school you couldn't study for the SAT's but in high school you could. You see? Everything is a step in the learning process.

Write one paragraph, then a page, then a chapter, then add another chapter, and another. There. Now you have a rough manuscript in the making. Get in writing groups. Let those who know the path share it with you.

The first time I made a pot of soup it was awful. I had to throw away the whole pot. It broke my heart. Every Saturday I tried the soup again. I practiced the art of soup making for months because soup is one of my favorite foods. Now I make soup without any doubt or feelings of insecurity. But I certainly didn't start out that way.

I used to make my own clothing and it took me decades to perfect the style I liked. I began to sew by hand, then bought a machine, then practiced combining patterns, then moved onto making my own patterns. Everything is a step by step learning process. Writing is no different but first we must overcome our own minds and realize that developing a skill to match our desire takes time, and practice, practice, practice.

The process of writing holds many challenges. We must allow ourselves to take the first step, then another, then another.

Pay attention to your mind, what it thinks and believes, and how it trips you up from getting started. What are your fears, what is the obstacle holding you back?

***You can write a book!***

*E.L. Doctorow said once said that 'Writing a novel is like driving a car at night. You can see only as far as your headlights, but you can make the whole trip that way.' You don't have to see where you're going, you don't have to see your destination or everything you will pass along the way. You just have to see two or three feet ahead of you. This is right up there with the best advice on writing, or life, I have ever heard.*

Anne Lamott

You've heard it said that if you want to make God laugh just tell him your plan. Writing a detailed outline for your book can be like that. Your characters won't do well if you confine them to who you think they should be. Take it one step at a time. Go to the corner – they will let you know if you should go straight or turn right. Let them have the reins – watch what they do – you might like what they want a whole lot better. Plan as much as you want but trust that somewhere along the path you will have to surrender your need for control.

Connect with other writers – it is so important to keep being reminded of the process. Being anal about having things your way only works when you arrange your socks.

*I never exactly made a book. It's rather like taking dictation.*
*I was given things to say.*

C.S. Lewis

Does the power of the written word come down from above or up from below, from the inside out or the outside in? It doesn't matter. Wherever the message comes from is somewhere holy and powerful.

Just write. That's all you have to do. Deal with the rest of the story when you have something on the page to deal with. Stories have a way of building their own momentum. You will know when you have enough information on paper. Then you edit.

Buy a new pen.  Watch how eager you'll be to use it if it's new. When we buy a new umbrella don't we wish for rain?

*The best time for planning a book is while you're doing the dishes.*

Agatha Christie

Once the mind is busy doing something else and the body is moving, the muse has freedom to move at her own pace. Our minds can stifle creativity by applying pressure to be creative. That pressure can stop the freedom of creativity cold in its track. No one can write effectively when this happens.

Sweeping, digging up weeds, painting a wall, fine tuning a guitar are meditative acts. Do them to quiet the mind. After you finish your chores don't be surprised if your muse leads you back to the blank paper.

Where else do you suppose she would take you?

*Writing a novel is a terrible experience, during which the hair often falls out and the teeth decay. I'm always irritated by people who imply that writing fiction is an escape from reality. It is a plunge into reality and it's very shocking to the system.*

Flannery O'Connor

Any writer who believes she can write anything other than reality is not paying attention.

Go ahead and write what you want. Just know that it won't escape reality, ever. What you write always has to relate to what people know and feel and experience.

Ideas lead to new ideas. You might just wind up writing a trilogy.

*I'm writing a book. I've got the page numbers done.*
Steven Wright


Page numbers are important so let's not criticize this first step. Ever drop your manuscript with unnumbered pages onto the floor? I have and it isn't pretty.

Even if you have to start with page numbers – start there.

Think about this: if you hadn't typed the page numbers first, you would have *nothing* written. Now keep going. Type the table of contents, the book title, and the About the Author page. Then go back and fill in the chapters.

Pick a town, what's it famous for, who lives there, does it have a favorite park? Will your story take place in this town?

Make a list of character defects. Will your characters have any of them?

What will your cover look like? Will it have pictures or just text?

Doing this to start with is a start. The very worst thing that could happen is that you get good at practicing structure.

*There are three rules for writing a novel. Unfortunately, no one knows what they are.*

W. Somerset Maugham

I'm asked frequently about what the best writing discipline is or when is the best time to write. I'm asked how one should begin to write a story and what is the best way to structure a book. Rules are what every lost writer wants to know. In many areas of our lives we want to learn how to get rid of rules. In writing, we hope that by knowing them we will get through our resistance.

When it comes to writing, don't bother asking anyone what the rules are. There aren't any. Every writer will tell you something different.

Listen to your instinct. When you get an inner sense that it is time to write, that is all you need to do. Then you can get busy finding out the rules and structure for grammar, story content, plot development, and the rest of it in a writing group.

*A good novel tells us the truth about its hero; but a bad novel tells us the truth about its author.*
G.K. Chesterton

Good writing is more than venting or throwing words on a page. So eventually you will want to learn the craft side of what you are doing.

Read everything you can get your hands on so you know the difference between something well-written and something that goes nowhere.

No writer wants to think about a reader sitting somewhere wondering why in the world she is wasting her time reading their book.

*You know, it's hard work to write a book. I can't tell you how many times I really get going on an idea, then my quill breaks. Or I spill ink all over my writing tunic.*
                                    Ellen DeGeneres


Don't forget to keep a sense of humor about your writing journey or the process can take you to hell.

If you hire an editor know that they are well-equipped soldiers set out to abuse your manuscript with slashes of red ink and streaks of penciled lines. They are jousters who can't wait to slice away unnecessary limbs.

Watch a funny movie, have a good laugh, a glass of wine, then get back to your manuscript and get your book completed.

*The reason that fiction is more interesting than any other form of literature, to those who really like to study people, is that in fiction the author can really tell the truth without humiliating himself.*

Eleanor Roosevelt


Therapists do it with sock puppets. Writers do it with characters. Being human is not easy and owning the shamefully vulnerable parts of who we are often takes tricking the mind.

That's where a good laugh with a friend is valuable.

Then oft your veil and pick up your pen. Give your painful story to a character and let them tell your story.

*I write to give myself strength. I write to be the characters that I am not. I write to explore all the things I'm afraid of.*
Joss Whedon

What a great way to describe hope. Writing is like giving yourself a second life. You live one life while you write another.  Hopefully the two will merge somewhere along the line.

Write your untold stories into a short story, poem, or journal entry.

If nothing else, this is good practice and might just lead to a novel.

**Why**

Who wants to live with a writer who
uses everything and everyone
as gist for the pen
always looking to create
from the ordinary?

Now, I ask you:
how else does a heart
breathe?


Jan Marquart
(published in *Cracked Open, A Book of Poems*, 2013)

# Question 6

**What happens when I know what I want to say but can't find the right words?**

Most people can't find the right words -- the first time.

Don't let this be a problem. Perhaps you won't start with the *right* words but you can start with *some* words. Then get busy finding more accurate words. This is called editing and you'll be doing it for a while. Editing is not a one-time deal; it happens over and over and over and over.

There is a difference between using a word that doesn't quite fit what you mean versus using the wrong word because of poor grammar. So memorize these and get on with writing. Maybe knowing these will be part of the solution.

1. *"Your" is possessive. "You're" is a contraction for "you are.*
2. *Apostrophes don't form plural nouns.*
3. *"There," "they're" and "their" are different words.*
4. *"Titled" is what you name your book. "Entitled" is a privilege.*
5. *The contraction "could have" is not written as "could of."*
6. *"To," "too," and "two" are also different words with different meanings.*
7. *"Its" is the possessive form of "it." "It's" is the contraction of "it is."*
8. *"Then" shows sequence of events. "Than" is used to compare nouns.*
9. *"Affect" is a verb and "effect" is a noun.*
10. *"Irony" does not mean "anything that is unexpected."*
11. *"Your seat belt is "loose." You "lose" your ice skates.*
12. *"Ensure" means to make sure of something. "Insure" is a way to get compensation for something.*

13. *"Literally" means exactly. "Figuratively" means metaphorically.*

Every artist should have the tools of her trade. Writers need a Dictionary and Thesaurus, pen and paper, internal sensations, visualizations, emotions, thoughts, and the senses. Beyond that go buy a book on grammar. Wherever your weakness is there is a book out there somewhere to help you. *Thank God for writers!*

*A memoir is only about what is already known.*
Nuala O'Faolain

.

*A scrupulous writer, in every sentence that he writes, will ask himself at least four questions, thus: 1. What am I trying to say? 2. What words will express it? 3. What image or idiom will make it clearer? 4. Is this image fresh enough to have an effect?*

George Orwell

These are great questions. You do not need to keep all the questions in mind at the same time. Start with the first one – write all you can on what you want to say.

The other questions have to do with editing. They come *after* the first writing.

This is the process.

*A non-writing writer is a monster courting insanity.*
                                    Franz Kafka


A story held captive without being released onto the page burns the temperament of someone who holds its power. Many writers will attest to the need to pay a lesson forward, whether it is told through a memoir or a novel.

Stories keep us connected to each other. They are the glue of humanity. We bond with people through stories.

Soldiers, for example, who suffer from PTSD and shut down from telling their stories because they are afraid of hurting the people close to them run the risk of imploding with anxiety, depression, suicidal thoughts, violence, or substance abuse. No one can hold a hand grenade whose pin has been pulled and spoon released and expect it not to explode.

If you meet any of these people, sit with an open heart and willing ears. You just might save a life. Then write and save your own. When emotions are ripe, words will flow.

*When you're missing a piece of yourself, aching, gut wrenching emptiness begins to take over. Until you find the link that completes your very soul, the feeling will never go away. Most people find a way to fill this void, material possessions, a string of relationships, affairs, food...I bear my soul, with words, for all to see.*

Jennifer Salaiz


Loss is a fragmenting experience. Talk therapy can help you understand what you are going through and help you cope and move on. But writing offers another benefit. Writing offers a way to internally bring all the fragments together so you can discover a new sense of self. Writing acknowledges that no part of life can ever be forgotten or left on the road. It must travel with you. Your task is to find a way to do that. Then you can build a new road for your journey with the power of words.

When losses are written their impact diminishes and their value increases. Use transitional words to describe these situations such as *realized, learned, understood, forgive.* These words help you grow because you found the courage to write.

Join a writing group and read everything you write.

*My bursting heart must find vent at my pen.*
                                    Abigail Adams


There are two times when people feel the need to pick up a pen and not think about too much about the 'right' words. One is when their hearts are full of love and the other is when their hearts are full of pain.

Isn't the pen a blessing?

*If I do not write to empty my mind, I go mad.*
George Gordon Byron


Just how much can one mind hold before it needs to be emptied?

For a writer everything is a story.

And sometimes finding the word that works best is a constant battle. There are too many words out there.

*If you want to change the world, pick up your pen and write.*
Martin Luther


Words are filled with power, that's why we have them for communication. Each word has its own energetic vibration and is designed to mean something specific. Have you read the US Constitution or the Bible or divorce papers? Each document has its own arrangement of words with a unique message.

Writing books is a great way to make your message run faster than fire.

*Ideas are like rabbits. You get a couple and learn how to handle them, and pretty soon you have a dozen.*
John Steinbeck

Writers are addicted to ideas because ideas lead to stories and stories lead to writing and writing leads to healing both the writer and reader. After witnessing the power of written stories, we must write and the more we want to write the more we need to write.

*I also want to say the dictionary, any unabridged dictionary, is a best. I read lists of words as though they were stories. Within their nuances, I see possibilities.*

Amy Tan

Open a dictionary and read down the page. How could you not desire to read on?

If you want a word a day coming to your inbox subscribe to www.wordsmith.org. Engross yourself in thinking about words so when you need them they are close by.

Remember when teachers used to give us new words to write in a sentence? Well use the daily word sent to your inbox from wordsmith and write a story about it. It's a great way to get a new idea for warming up your creative juices.

# Question 7

**What do I do when I can't find anything to write about?**

There will be days when you feel like writing and actually have time to write but nothing comes to mind.

So don't sit there and suffer. Get up and do something to get your muse stimulated.

Ride a bus – Buses are full of interesting people. Talk to them, ask them about their lives. If you don't feel inclined to speak to strangers, look for the weirdest, most conservative looking, loudest, or coolest and write a creative story about that character. You can also write the opposite. Take someone who looks dull and make up an interesting story about his life.

Bookstores – Pick up any book and read the first sentence. Then write your own story from there. You can look for a strange characteristic or mannerism about someone and capitalize on it.

Once I was browsing the sale table at B&N in Santa Fe. A young man around twenty, dressed from head to toe in black with rings everywhere, tattoos up his arms and black hair spiked in a tall Mohawk stood in front of me. He appeared tough and rebellious. I watched him for a few minutes then put my attention back on the sale books.

About ten minutes later I looked up. He was sitting on a tiny foot stool holding an infant dressed in light pink with a small pink bow wrapped around her forehead. He stared into her eyes and spoke softly to her. It was the most beautiful scene. I had to fight back tears. The persona he expressed holding that baby was so opposite to what he portrayed while just standing there looking tough. I couldn't wait to get to my paper to write about him. It was one of those moments when first impressions get so fully corrected and activate your mind.

Over the years I've had many first impressions turn out to be false. Write them – they are powerful.

*Write what should not be forgotten.*
Isabel Allende

Courage, survival, triumph, love, persistence, endurance, forgiveness, faith, creativity, devotion, loyalty, these are the experiences we need to write about. Writing is the perfect way to make stories immortal. We must not forget what really matters, that secrets keep us sick, love can be both a blessing and a curse, and that generations of humans have thrived by overcoming.

Connect with memories that contribute to the power of being human. Those stories should never be forgotten for they are the answers for the next generations.

*I write differently from what I speak, I speak differently from what I think, I think differently from the way I ought to think, and so it all proceeds into deepest darkness.*

Franz Kafka

The more you write, the more you find out about the voice inside you. Follow it. It speaks even when your mouth is silent. Write it.

*A person is a fool to become a writer. His only compensation is absolute freedom. He has no master except his own soul, and that, I am sure, is why he does it.*

Roald Dahl

Lady Ga Ga and Cher put on stage what writers want to put on paper: creativity, authenticity, and the freedom of telling a story.

Find your personal limitations then take them a step further. Go where others do not dare go.

Boldly take on being an iconoclastic thinker.

Rebelliousness fuels the pen.

*The good writers touch life often. The mediocre ones run a quick hand over her. The bad ones rape her and leave her for the flies.*

Ray Bradbury

Readers read to understand the parts of life they don't understand. They want writers to be their heroes and they trust them to reveal the wisdom they are too afraid to learn for themselves. Readers want proof that there is a way out of conflict, to find love, to become successful. They yearn to understand their own grief, sadness, and suffering. Fantasy is wonderful but even fantasy has to have a true emotional content. If characters of fantasy do not resemble the truth about life no one will believe them.

Readers not only want to hold hands with the writer when they jump into the deep end, readers also want writers to throw them a life raft. They want to hear how life really is and how they can be saved from it. They do not want to hear lies about what they are living and trust me, readers know when writers are lying.

Write a salvation story.

Find writers who have written what you love to read and stay close to them. Read everything they have written.

Then write for yourself.

*Write what disturbs you, what you fear, what you have not been willing to speak about. Be willing to be split open.*
Natalie Goldberg

Without becoming cracked open, where can we enter, what can come out? How can we understand ourselves, our world, our relationships if we don't examine the smallest crevice?

Where else would you expect to meet your authentic self if not in the space of a crack?

What would come out if you were cracked open? What brings you to your knees? What are you pushing back from the space between feeling and revealing?

That's where you start.

*Every secret of a writer's soul, every experience of his life, every quality of his mind, is written large in his works.*
Virginia Woolf

Read authors carefully because each one will show you how to write and how to recreate your own story. Memoirs, fiction, non-fiction, creative non-fiction, poems, short stories – all authors in all genres show you the way.

Each day you live moments worthy of a story. Write about one of them. Just pick *one*.

*Writing is not necessarily something to be ashamed of, but do it in private and wash your hands afterwards.*

Robert A. Heinlein

Writing deeply means revealing deep secrets, vulnerabilities, and pain. Writers cannot predict what will show up on the page once they start writing stream of consciousness.

When the writing begins, step out of the way and become a witness to that which gets exposed. Do not stop the pen. The good, the bad, and the ugly each need their turn.

The rawest of human experiences has lots to say – write it out in the privacy of your bedroom then take it to the living room, then an agent.

*Why does one begin to write? Because she feels
misunderstood, I guess. Because it never comes out clearly
enough when she tries to speak. Because she wants to
rephrase the world, to take it in and give it back again
differently, so that everything is used and nothing is lost.*

Nicole Krauss

Writing gives you the opportunity to know your mind,
your heart, the way you want others to know your story.
Everyone feels misunderstood at some point and writers
get to explain themselves without anyone interrupting.

There is no need to fight someone eye to eye to get him to
believe who you are. Write, put it out there, then walk
away.

What do you want people to know about you? The answer
can't be *nothing*. You have a whole world alive inside you.

*Make up a story... For our sake and yours forget your name in the street; tell us what the world has been to you in the dark places and in the light. Don't tell us what to believe, what to fear. Show us belief's wide skirt and the stitch that unravels fear's caul.*

Toni Morrison

Bring the world to its knees - then write a path to show readers how to stand up.

*A writer is someone for whom writing is more difficult than it is for other people.*

Thomas Mann

A true writer cares about each word painstakingly making sure that what burns to be said is without doubt on the page.

Write about why writing is difficult for you then make it an article and submit it.

# Question 8

**What do I do with what I write?**

Most writers don't know what to do with their finished manuscripts.

Today there are thousands of options.

Network with published authors because they have already walked the process.

Keep in mind that whether authors are self-published or traditionally published, they have done something with their manuscripts.

Online journals are wonderful for getting published.

Magazines are great steps to getting published without having to write long pieces and best of all most of them pay.

Pick up a copy of the *Writer's Market* and check out all the places where you can get published.

Go to local writing groups and see where other writers have had written pieces accepted.

*You must keep sending work out; you must never let a manuscript do nothing but eat its head off in a drawer. You send that work out again and again, while you're working on another one. If you have talent, you will receive some measure of success - but only if you persist.*

Isaac Asimov

Do you really think that the cliché *the squeaky wheel gets the oil* is just a fairy tale? Just don't keep sending out the same manuscript if an agent tells you it is flawed. If given advice on how to make a manuscript better, take it.

View rejections as a learning curve and not a statement that you shouldn't write. Writing each day is practice. Everything you write is practice for the next project. Persist, persist, and persist some more.

Then next time your manuscript might get accepted.

*Writing isn't about making money, getting famous, getting dates, getting laid, or making friends. In the end, it's about enriching the lives of those who will read your work, and enriching your own life, as well. It's about getting up, getting well, and getting over. Getting happy, okay? Getting happy.*
Stephen King

Write about your life. When you write about your life you make it count for something and those who read what you have written will believe that their lives amount to something too.

Write the stories that make your life interesting so others can view life as interesting as well.

No fragmented experience is unnecessary. All of it counts as one life.

Then find a venue for your written work. Make it count.

*After writing a story I was always empty and both sad and happy, as though I had made love.*
                    Ernest Hemingway


The wholeness writers feel after they boldly tell their stories is one of the most intimate feelings a writer can experience.

Finishing a story is like finally answering the last question of a four hour exam. Suddenly you cannot remember anything. You have let it all go. You are spent and it is exhilarating.

Go to book signings. Talk to authors who have finally released their stories to the world. Listen to them. Then go home and write more.

Make booklets of your stories and give them out as holiday presents.

*I wrote so as simply to live, and then so as to live better, and not just to get better at managing life, but to be a better person.*

Nuala O'Faolain

# Question 9

**What kind of writing discipline should I use?**

Let's say you have a full day of errands but a friend calls and says that Nordstrom's is having a great sale and you just have to go to it. You look at your day to see what chores you can eliminate so you can take advantage of the sale. Finally you just drop everything and go shopping. When you are through with the sales, you start on your errands again. That's what setting a writing discipline is like. No matter what, you write. Nothing stops you – you write.

Questions about the discipline of writing come up everywhere there are writers. The belief that a writing discipline is needed is partly true. If you don't write – well – you don't write.

Some writers wait for inspiration and then they write. Some go to their desks every day to show up and write.

Tolstoy dictated his books to his daughter while on his deathbed. That is a true writer. How badly do you want to write? How badly did you want to go to the Nordstrom sale?

Authors have 24 hours in the day just like everyone else. Bookstores are full of books written by busy people that made the time to get books completed. You can do it too.

*The most valuable of all talents is that of never using two words when one will do.*
Thomas Jefferson

It is a fallacy to think that you need every word of every sentence in every paragraph on every page. Writers despise getting rid of words they spent much time to find. But then again, all hoarders keep the things they don't need. It is okay to spring clean your story.

Write out your story. Count the words. Cut the word count in half and edit to match that number. Cut that number in half again and edit again to match that number. Keep doing it until no more words can be omitted and what you will have left is a tightly written story.

Enter writing contests that require a limited word count. Edit. Edit. Edit. This is a fabulous discipline for learning about the use of language. Only use words that contribute to the story. If they are superfluous, omit them.

Then go eat chocolate.

*Put down everything that comes into your head and then you're a writer. But an author is one who can judge his own stuff's worth, without pity, and destroy most of it.*

Colette

Writing and the craft of writing are as different as ice cream and the ingredients that go into it. If you want to create a new flavor of ice cream you must experiment with new ingredients. What doesn't add to the flavor must be removed. It is the same with words and their stories.

Let the unnecessary and unneeded go into the trash. Most writing is warm up anyway. It takes discipline to let go and not mourn over cutting out sentences you might have struggled weeks to create.

Train your mind to keep only what is needed.

*We have to continually be jumping off cliffs and developing our wings on the way down.*
                                              Kurt Vonnegut


Do not give up.

I once knew an historical novelist who became quite depressed when his agent said it wasn't time for an historical novel. One night he got drunk and angry and believing his agent's words threw his novel into the fireplace and watched it burn. This was before computers. He had no copy of it.

If you aren't happy with your agent go find another agent. I mentioned before that JK Rowling was turned down 12 times. This is more the norm for writers than not. Rejections are ways for a writer to develop strong and resilient wings. What choice do we have if we don't want to splatter ourselves on the rocks?

Put a Band-Aid on your elbow and go out and laugh with other writers who have worse stories than you to tell. Once you see that rejections are normal you'll just move on, as you should if you want to be published. Discipline yourself to keep hope in your work.

*Cram your head with characters and stories. Abuse your library privileges. Never stop looking at the world, and never stop reading to find out what sense other people have made of it. If people give you a hard time and tell you to get your nose out of a book, tell them you're working. Tell them it's research. Tell them to pipe down and leave you alone.*
Jennifer Weiner

The world is full of mediocre minds that focus on TV and microwaved food thinking convenience is all there is to an exciting life. They don't know the fullness of a soul after a story is written or the excitement of readers eager to turn the next page in your book.

The written word thrills both the one who put it on paper and the one who found the paper.

Discipline yourself to keep reading books by authors in all genres. This practice will stretch your mind and keep you open to possibilities for your stories when it is your time to write.

*Don't bend; don't water it down; don't try to make it logical; don't edit your own soul according to the fashion. Rather, follow your most intense obsessions mercilessly.*
Franz Kafka

Don't appease anyone. We are made with distinct differences and when we try to be like everyone else, write like everyone else, live like everyone else, we suffer.

The force that drives us does so for a reason. We must live it and work with it until we learn from it so we can do what must be done with it. Write it out. Writing is a way to learn who we are.

The discipline of self-honoring is difficult. It can become all too easy to doubt and give up on ourselves. Writers cannot do this. This is writer-suicide.

Join book clubs and keep reading.

*All I need is a sheet of paper*
*and something to write with, and then*
*I can turn the world upside down.*
                    Friedrich Nietzsche


Who said writers have no power? Look how much power
the written words of Thomas Jefferson and Webster have.

Stay connected to those who write and watch pens turn
into magic wands. The discipline of writing makes sure you
have the tools of the trade handy.

Get in the habit of keeping pads and pens in all the rooms
in your house. When an idea strikes – you are ready.

Then go change your world.

*Write. Rewrite. When not writing or rewriting, read. I know of no shortcuts.*

Larry L. King

That's because there aren't any. Times like this require fearlessness, persistence, and perseverance.

Write – read – write – read – write – read. Can you think of a better discipline for the mind of a writer?

*I do not over-intellectualize the production process. I try to keep it simple: Tell the damned story.*

Tom Clancy

If you expect your thoughts to come out exactly as the final editing you will be sorely mistaken.

Sit and write and don't give a thought to anything else.

The discipline to keep the story moving is an important one. If you wander off track the mind might be taking you somewhere important or it might be sidetracking you to steal your attention. How long do you let yourself get lost on the freeway? Always have the discipline to get back on the road.

*I don't need an alarm clock. My ideas wake me.*
                    Ray Bradbury


New mothers have infants to awaken them at 3 in the
morning for a feeding. The writer has the muse. It is as
simple as that.

Get in the habit of keeping a pen and book light by your
bed so you don't have to turn on the light in the dark.
Discipline yourself to awaken long enough to write the
ideas that woke you up because I promise you they will be
gone in the morning.

*Writer's block is a condition that affects amateurs and people who aren't serious about writing. So is the opposite, namely inspiration, which amateurs are also very fond of. Putting it another way: a professional writer is someone who writes just as well when they're not inspired as when they are.*

Philip Pullman

There is no such thing as writer's block. Listen – what you are feeling is the mind trying to get your attention. The inner voice is always talking. Listen. That's all you have to do.

As far as inspiration is concerned, it makes cameo appearances when it pleases. Meanwhile you still have to attend to your story.

Discipline yourself to write whether inspiration makes a visit or not. If your mind is stuck move your body. Nothing is lost. Just listen, take care of yourself, then write.

*I wish craziness and foolishness and madness upon you. May you live with hysteria, and out of it make fine stories — science fiction or otherwise. Which finally means, may you be in love every day for the next 20,000 days. And out of that love, remake a world.*

Ray Bradbury


Isn't this beautiful? What does it mean? Well I suppose you'll have to write to find out. Then share it with other writers. The only way we know the process – is to do it.

Writers often believe that their thoughts have to be logical or academic in order to write something of value. Get into the discipline of allowing your mind to venture off. Look how doing that served JK Rowling.

Free the pen.

*You can't wait for inspiration. You have to go after it with a club.*

Jack London

Stories die waiting for inspiration. Insist they get on the page.

Don't give up. This is a discipline that is the most difficult. Taking action to write something each day feels like you are going against the grain. Perhaps you are but at least at the end of the day you have written *something*.

*Lock up your libraries if you like; but there is no gate, no lock, no bolt that you can set upon the freedom of my mind.*
Virginia Woolf


Everyone strives for freedom, even in America. But the pen has no bars to it. It desires freedom. It allows freedom. It gives you all the space you need.

Do a free write daily. That is a great discipline for giving the mind freedom.

Let it run in the meadows.

*But as far as writing was concerned, I was floundering, trying to write detective novels like Edgar Wallace and espionage novels like E. Phillips Oppenheim. I tried to imitate them. I simply didn't know that my own experiences were of any value. Nobody told us anything about that. No teacher eve said, "Go home and write about your family."*

Frank McCourt

Writer after writer keeps saying that it is our own lives that have the most power when we write. Guess they are on to something.

If you set a discipline to write one family story a week your writing will change. When you write about something you know deep within it holds more passion and readers love that.

*I wish I had a secret I could let you in on, some formula my father passed on to me in a whisper just before he died, some code word that has enabled me to sit at my desk and land flights of creative inspiration like an air-traffic controller. But I don't. All I know is that the process is pretty much the same for almost everyone I know.*

Anne Lamott

We all want the secrets to success. But there is no secret. There is only the unraveling until we find ourselves.

We all do this. And writers do their fair share of unraveling in order to wake up what is inside them.

Writing regularly, with discipline and conviction, eventually leads to success. There is no other path to it.

**When I Die**

Remember to put a pen in my hand
as I take my last breath
so I can set my stories free
and finish my life's dance on earth.

It makes no sense to take these stories with me.

I do not like loose ends.

They are for you.

Jan Marquart
(published in *Cracked Open, A Book of Poems*, 2013)

# Question 10

**Now that I've finished my manuscript how do I deal with those who are critical of it?**

It depends – who is the critic?

Is the critic someone who doesn't like what you wrote? Tell him to write his own book.

Is the critic someone who doesn't like your writing style? Tell him to write his own book.

Is the critic an agent who is willing to give you advice to make the book better? Take her advice.

Is the critic your own mind? Tell it to shut up.

Remember: you are the author. You get to make the decisions for the book's well-being. But don't throw the baby out with the shampoo just because you absolutely love each word and character and detail you have created. This is a slippery slope. Some advice is going to be worthy of consideration.

If you get good advice, take it. If you get shamed for telling your story, walk away.

*I went for years not finishing anything. Because, of course, when you finish something you can be judged.*
Erica Jong


Fear – Shame - Guilt.

These emotions are death to a writer.

What are you afraid of?

Do you feel badly that you wrote something because someone doesn't like it?

Have you done something wrong?

It doesn't matter what the answers are. Your stories are still worthy.

Not one emotion escapes the experience of being human, not even for one human being.

*Get it down. Take chances. It may be bad, but it's the only way you can do anything really good.*
William Faulkner

We cannot edit anything that isn't written.

You are allowed to write the worst crap. If you have a bad manuscript you can throw it away confident that you can write a better one the second time. At least you know you were able to overcome the list of fears, obstacles, and days of non-writing. A writer has to start somewhere. So when you write it – write it boldly and keep going.

Remember the statistics in the beginning of this book? Consider yourself a member of an elite group. It is always the ones who venture from the pack that get the most condemnation. Ever study the psychology of group think?

*It is the writer who might catch the imagination of young people, and plant a seed that will flower and come to fruition.*

Isaac Asimov

It's been said that a writer should know its audience. On some level that is an impossible task. Books germinate like seeds.

Writers change the world one page and one reader at a time.

With the billions of people on the planet I don't think it wise to concern yourself with one or two people who are anti-imagination, do you?

*Writing is its own reward.*

Henry Miller

Until you find a way to make lots of money from your books, enjoy the process, which I suspect, has changed you into a more authentic human being.

Anyone who criticizes you for writing is only giving you their reaction. You can still hold onto the feeling of joy that has erupted inside you. Maybe in new moments you can teach your friend the reward of writing.

Here is an excerpt from an interview with Jan Marquart, CEO and Founder of About the Author Network, by Lisa Shirah-Hiers, which was published in Vol. 17, No. 3, September, 2013 in the *Story Circle Journal*. www.storycircle.org

*1)  How did you become both a writer and a therapist?*

JM: I was born in Brooklyn and lived there until I decided to go to college in California. I quit a great job as a legal secretary on Wall Street which disturbed my parents, but I couldn't see myself taking shorthand and typing someone else's ideas forever. I wanted to find out what *I* thought and desired to write since I was eight but tucked it away when my parents didn't show an interest. When I enrolled in UCSC I met a friend who recommended I keep a journal. I have written every day since June 1972. I studied philosophy and then got my masters in social work.

*2) What are some other accomplishments you are most proud of?*

JM: No matter what anyone said about me I always worked to believe in myself. I healed two illnesses doctors said I couldn't. I have owned three homes in the last 30 years and never missed a mortgage payment, even when the financial challenges were great and everyone around me said I couldn't do it without a husband. I have made a conscious effort to remain kind and caring towards others because I learned that no matter what it seems, there is always a backdrop to every life.

*3) What do you wish people knew about you?*

JM: That is a great question. I have felt misunderstood most of my life and I realized that the thinking many people do is so limited and fearful. I suppose that's why I write so much. When the pressure builds inside me I have to say it somehow, through some genre and still keep hope and faith. It takes a lot for me to ask for help, not because I can't ask but because I don't believe my life's problems belong to anyone but me. I'd like people to know that for anyone who is suffering, me or anyone else, to receive an offer of help restores faith in humanity.

4) Do you think fiction is harder than non-fiction? Why or why not?

JM: Not really. In non-fiction you really have to know what you're talking about or you come off as an idiot. So when I write non-fiction I do lots of research and work to get all my ducks in a row before I publish. Fiction, on the other hand, shows me a way to have more fun with writing. I realized half-way into the manuscript of Kate's Way and half-way into The Basket Weaver, that I could design any ending I wanted. In non-fiction that is not a luxury. Readers of non-fiction are counting on facts. Kate's Way and The Basket Weaver started out serious in that they started out with something I wanted to address or heal in my life. Then it came time to create an ending and I realized the ending was only going to come about if I molded it the way I wanted. So it was like finger painting and pushing color into new spaces.

5) What advice would you give to beginning writers?

JM: Don't worry about how to discipline yourself to write. Don't worry about whether you can write or not. If you have something to say simply say it. You can't edit or publish anything unless you have written something first. I hear writers tell me in my workshops how frightened they are that someone they love will be angry at what they write. In my experience too many people don't do what they desire because of the criticism of narrow-minded and fear-based people. This is a dangerous place for writers. Write. Let other people decide how to behave around what you wrote.

*6) Evidence for and trusting one's own intuition seems to be a major theme in much of your writing. Can you speak a little about that?*

JM: In the last twenty something years I had quite a few people tell me I couldn't do some things while something inside me told me I could. They thought I just wanted to battle with them but I wasn't battling. I wasn't being recalcitrant. I truly knew I could do what they said I couldn't and proceeded from there. Turns out I did everything others told me I couldn't. So when people tell me what they think I am or am not capable of doing something, I listen to the message from my gut. Sometimes my gut agrees and sometimes it doesn't. When I know better and I rationalize a reason not to listen to that voice, I suffer terribly. Listen to everyone but rarely take their comments to heart, especially when it comes to your capability.

*7) Describe your own journey to find your voice. What were some obstacles along the way? How did you overcome them? Is it still challenging?*

JM: My own journey was far more difficult than I could have ever imagined. In The Breath of Dawn I wrote about a near-death illness that presented me with a great challenge to heal if I wanted to get on with my life after doctors said it wasn't possible. In 2000 I was over-exposed to Black Mold and environmental illness (MCS) developed as a result. Again five doctors said I was the sickest woman they ever met but had no clue about what to do for me. They were grim about having any recovery. The only thing my mind held onto during the entire time of one loss after another was something T.D. Jakes said in one of his shows:

When God Strips You Down to Nothing – He's Up to Something. If I didn't believe there was a purpose to all the suffering I went through I don't know if I could have survived. My poems address much of what I learned through that time in *Cracked Open* even though I did not feel the need to regurgitate the actual traumatic events. That will come someday, I expect.

*8) Do you have a favorite quote? What is it?*

JM: I have many. I love this one by Thoreau: *If one advances confidently in the direction of their dreams, and endeavors to live the life they've imagined, they will meet success unexpected in common hours.*

## About the Interviewer

Lisa Shirah-Hiers earned a Bachelor's Degree in Music Theory/Composition *summa cum laude* from Lawrence University, Appleton, Wisconsin and a Master's Degree in Composition from UT Austin. A former classical radio announcer on Austin's KMFA, she now pursues a double career in writing and music, teaching piano, theory and composition as well as facilitating writing workshops (often incorporating music). She has published numerous articles for the *Hill Country Sun* and *Austinwoman* and is a contributing editor to the *Story Circle Journal*. She serves on the board of the Story Circle Network, a women's life-writing organization, and is a member of the Music Teacher's Association, the Texas and Austin District Music Teacher Associations and the Writer's League of Texas.

Authors quoted in this book are listed below.

Rachel Naomi Remen
Epictetus
Aleister Crowley
Stephen King
Ernest Hemingway
Neil Gaiman
Kurt Vonnegut
Cornelia Funke
Margaret Atwood
Tennessee Williams
Gloria Steinem
Jules Renard
Dylan Thomas
Rainer Maria Rilke
Oscar Wilde
Robert Frost
Cyril Connolly
Buddha
Amy Tan
Julia Cameron
Carl Sagan
Ursula LeGuin
Virginia Woolf
Ray Bradbury
Jarold Kintz
Paula Coelho
Isaac Asimov
Lloyd Alexander
Vladimir Nabokov
Joan Didion
Anais Nin
Maya Angelou
Nuala O'Faolain

Alice Koller
Somerset Maugham
Anne Lamott
C.S. Lewis
Agatha Christie
Flannery O'Connor
Steven Wright
G. K. Chesterton
Ellen DeGeneres
Eleanor Roosevelt
Joss Whedon
George Orwell
Franz Kafka
Jennifer Solaiz
Abigail Adams
George Gordon Byron
Martin Luther
John Steinbeck
Isabel Allende
Ronald Dahl
Natalie Goldberg
Virginia Woolf
Robert A. Heinlein
Nicole Krauss
Toni Morrison
Thomas Mann
Thomas Jefferson
Colette
Jennifer Weiner
Friedrich Nietzsche
Larry King
Tom Clancy
Phillip Pullman

Jack London

Frank McCourt

Jimmy Santiago Baca

Erica Jong

William Faulkner

Henry Miller

My deepest thanks to each of these writers. They are inspirational human beings.

The world is better off because of their courage, perseverance, and determination to write about their creative stories and experiences.

## ABOUT THE AUTHOR

**Jan Marquart** has loved writing since she was eight years old. She has published eleven books, two booklets, poems, short stories, and essays on healing and life. She is an avid reader and encourages reading, especially for those wanting to be a writer.

In her psychotherapy practice Jan uses writing as a modality for healing and has helped women all around the world overcome emotional, physical, and experiential stress. Jan has healed many of her own health problems through the use of her pen and has written 96 daily journals.

Jan's project **About the Author Network** is for writers, authors, and professional resources that support the writing community. Her interest is to make sure no writer stands alone. Every writer needs support and encouragement and it is Jan's desire to make sure writers can lean on like-minded individuals to get projects completed.

Everyone has a story and Jan believes that no one should die without sharing their stories with the world.

Jan can be reached at:

jan_marquart@yahoo.com,
www.AboutTheAuthorNetwork.com
www.JanMarquart.com
www.JanMarquartlcsw.wordpress.com
www.AwareLivingNow.blogspot.com
www.FreethePen.wordpress.com
https://www.facebook.com/jan.marquart.16


**To book Jan Marquart for a speaking engagement about writing, contact her at:**
**jan_marquart@yahoo.com**

*Because solitude is an achievement.*

Alice Koller

NOTES

NOTES

NOTES

# NOTES

NOTES

NOTES

NOTES